Preparing for the Praxis Exams

Rodney Estrada

Merrill
Prentice Hall

Upper Saddle River, New Jersey
Columbus, Ohio

Point Park University
Education Department, 710 AH
201 Wood Street
Pittsburgh, PA 15222-1984

Vice President and Publisher: Jeffery W. Johnston
Acquisitions Editor: Debra A. Stollenwerk
Production Editor: JoEllen Gohr
Design Coordinator: Diane C. Lorenzo
Cover Designer: Thomas Borah
Production Manager: Pamela D. Bennett
Director of Marketing: Ann Castel Davis
Marketing Manager: Krista Groshong
Marketing Coordinator: Tyra Cooper

Pearson Education Ltd.
Pearson Education Australia Pty. Limited
Pearson Education Singapore Pte. Ltd.
Pearson Education North Asia Ltd.
Pearson Education Canada, Ltd.
Pearson Educación de Mexico, S.A. de C.V.
Pearson Education—Japan
Pearson Education Malaysia Pte. Ltd.
Pearson Education, *Upper Saddle River, New Jersey*

ETS and Praxis are registered trademarks of the Educational
Testing Service. All efforts have been made to maintain the
integrity and confidentiality of the Praxis Series exams
and questions.

Merrill
Prentice Hall

10 9 8 7 6 5 4 3 2 1
ISBN: 0-13-097315-7

Dedication

*To my wife Stephanie, with whom all things are possible.
And to my children, Claire, Conner, Alison, and Jacob,
who keep me humble.*

Contents

Chapter 1

Introduction to the Praxis

Praxis Overview

If you are preparing for or considering a career in education, you will most likely be required to take a certification test called Praxis. Praxis consists of, in most cases, a series of exams: Praxis I, Praxis II and Praxis III. The three exams correspond to the three milestones in teacher development: entering into teacher education, receipt of certification, and in-service instruction. The word Praxis comes from the theory base and simply means reflective process. This test is designed to assess your ability to think through a process of pedagogy and make responses to issues of content or instruction.

Praxis I is designed for students entering into teacher education programs and for individuals with degrees seeking initial teacher certification from their states. Praxis I assesses students' basic knowledge of mathematics, reading skills and writing skills, typically to the eighth grade level. The Praxis I is usually taken prior to entry into teacher education programs or prior to entry into junior and senior level education courses.

Praxis II assesses students' knowledge of content and pedagogy for the actual content area in which they are seeking certification. With this test students may, for instance, be tested on the knowledge required to teach their grade levels and/or content areas. In addition, knowledge of pedagogic ability is assessed for some testing areas. The Praxis II is usually taken in the semester immediately prior to graduation or post graduation. University requirements may vary so check with your advisor.

Praxis III is an in-service test typically given to first-year postcertified or precertified teachers in the classroom setting. Based on established guidelines, Educational Testing Service (ETS) evaluators come to a classroom and evaluate a first-year teacher on instruction and ability. This assessment determines the level and capability of the instructor and is used as a predictor of future success and eventual certification. While this test is not used in all states, it is being used in a growing number of states throughout the Praxis network.

This book focuses on Praxis I and II and provides the potential Praxis test taker with test-taking strategies and study tips, as well as specific strategies on taking and passing the Praxis I and II exams.

Getting Started

First, you must determine if you are required to take the Praxis exams. Second, you must discover which specific exams for your content area you need to take, and the passing requirements for each exam.

Each exam is labeled with a title and a code. For example, exams for elementary education testing in the state of Georgia are titled Content Area Exercises, testing code 20012 and Curriculum Instruction and Assessment, testing code 10016.

Every state uses a different exam with different passing requirements. Determine which testing code applies to your content area and the score needed to meet your state's passing requirements. You want to make sure that each exam you take is relevant to certification for your content area in your state.

State by state requirements for Praxis testing can be found by:
- Contacting your university or college certification office.
- Contacting your teacher certification board.
- Accessing the Educational Testing Service (ETS) Registration Bulletin or the ETS web site at www.teachingandlearning.org. (The inside front cover of the bulletin lists phone numbers of state teacher certification board offices.)

To begin your relationship with the Educational Testing Service, obtain a copy of the Praxis Registration Bulletin, or contact them at 609-771-7395. You may also visit their web site at www.ets.org/teachingandlearning.org/ for updates on testing requirements and other relevant information.

Whom Should You Contact?

Direct certification questions to your college certification officer or the state certifying board. They should be able to answer questions concerning what your state requires for teacher certification.

ETS can help you with questions about registration, score verification, study guide purchases, and other issues regarding your test.

ETS Services

It is very important to take advantage of the services ETS offers, both before and during your testing experience.

- A service the ETS provides that you may find useful is "scores by phone." This allows you to receive your scores earlier than the regular scores by mail process. Refer to the registration bulletins index under "scores by phone" for a calendar indicating when your test scores will be available after your test date.

- A second service you may want to consider is the score verification service. Students who fail their test by one to five points should consider using this ETS service. If you receive a score verification report in which your scores come back lower or higher, there is no charge for the service. If your score stays the same, there is a charge. Again, refer to the registration bulletin for the specific charge for the test you might consider having verified.

- The ETS provides free study materials for your test, called *Tests at a Glance (TAAG)*, and other ETS-prepared materials such as study guides. Students who review or purchase these materials will be well prepared; many of the questions in the *TAAG* or study guides resemble or precisely reflect questions on the Praxis exam. Contact ETS at http://www.ets.org/teachingand learning/ or at 609-771-7395.

Chapter 2

Praxis I

Praxis I Overview

The first test in the Praxis Series is the Praxis I. This is a pre-test usually given to students prior to entry into teacher education programs. It consists of three one-hour-long tests, one each for Reading, Writing and Mathematics. It is designed to assess your basic competencies in these areas.

Do You Need to Take the Praxis I?

Again, as with all Praxis testing, you need to first find out if your state requires Praxis I. If so, determine which Praxis I tests you need to take, and at what time during your education process you are required to take them. Some states require Praxis I testing of all people seeking initial certification. Some states only require it for entry into teacher certification programs, and other states do not require it at all.

Which Form Should You Take?

The ETS is phasing out the old CBT form of testing. As of January 1, 2002 the CBT test will no longer be given anywhere. However, there will still be two forms of testing—the Pre-Professional Skills Test (PPST) and the new Computer-Based Pre-Professional Skills Test (CBT-PPST).

The PPST form of the test is just another paper and pencil form of testing. The test is given on the same six test days as all other Praxis exams (except in the state of Louisiana). The CBT-PPST is given at computer labs on college campuses, at

Sylvan Learning Centers, and at other computer-based labs around the country. You can take the test once every sixty days and the cost can range from $95 for the PPST to $130 for the CBT-PPST. The CBT-PPST requires a different registration bulletin than the PPST.

The CBT-PPST is exactly like the PPST only it is taken on a computer. Students are permitted to review questions, and are given a single essay question. A calculator is no longer needed. Actual content and styles of questions are the same on the paper and computer versions.

If you find reading challenging, or struggle with reading from a computer screen, you may not want to take the computer-based form of the test. Research has shown that reading from a computer screen can decrease overall reading comprehension.

Exemptions from the Praxis I

In some Praxis states, there may be exemptions that allow students to opt out of taking the Praxis I. These exemptions vary from state to state and students may want to ask their college certification officer or state teacher certification board the following question:

- Is there an SAT, ACT, MAT or GRE score that can exempt me from taking the Praxis I? In some states, for instance, a minimum score of 1000 on the SAT, with a score of 480 on the Verbal component and a score of 520 on the Quantitative component, will exempt a student from taking the Praxis I exam.

Passing the Praxis I

Passing the Praxis I test can be accomplished in one of three ways:

- Minimum scores: Are there initial minimum scores for each test for your state that you must meet? For instance, passing scores of 177 on the Writing portion, 176 on the Reading portion and 174 on the Mathematics portion are minimum scores.

- Composite scores: Can you count a composite score? For instance, if you take the Reading, Writing and Mathematics portions and fail only the Mathematics portion, some states allow you to add the three existing scores for a composite score, thus allowing you to pass the test without retaking the failed portion.

- A concordance: Does my state allow for a concordance to be used to calculate composite scores if I have taken the test on computer (CBT) or in paper form (PPST)? The concordance is a table your state teacher certification board or college certification officer uses to make comparisons of your various testing sessions and their passing and failing scores. Essentially, your CBT scores are turned into PPST scores and recalculated to find a new composite score, and vice versa. This process must be done by your certification officer or state certifying board.

Praxis I Strategies

Now let's look at what to study and discuss some strategies you could employ in preparing for this test. Let's first examine the content of the test. The Praxis I is a test of Mathematics, Reading Comprehension and Writing Skills.

Mathematics

In the Mathematics section, you will be asked sixty multiple choice questions and have sixty minutes in which to answer them. This section covers material through the eighth grade. It is material that you have certainly studied in your education life; however, you may not have seen this material since the eighth grade. For instance, you might be asked to:

- Identify the isosceles triangle out of a lineup of several different triangles.

- Determine what 6/32 of 79 equals.

- Do some simple algebraic solution solving.

These are easy questions, but you will have to refresh yourself on those basics. For the Mathematics section I recommend the following preparation strategies:

- *LearningPlus* is a software tutorial specifically designed for the Praxis I. It is usually supported at universities and colleges with teacher certification programs. Barring the software, the *LearningPlus* manuals can be purchased at bookstores all over the country. *LearningPlus* in its computer form is a tutorial/timed test all in one. It is, bar none, the best study guide you can acquire for your Praxis I preparation.

- Seventh or eighth grade mathematics textbooks are useful for study. They can be obtained at local schools, libraries and school boards. Spend time working the problems and refreshing your ability to perform this level of mathematics.

- Other study guides on the market may be helpful. Publishers include Baron's, Arco and the Educational Testing Service.

The goal with all of these materials is to review and drill, then review and drill some more. Work as many problems as possible, and spend time relearning this basic math that you may have forgotten over the years.

Reading Comprehension

The Reading Comprehension section consists of forty questions to be answered in sixty minutes. As you approach the Reading Comprehension portion of the test, you want to first go to the current *Tests at a Glance (TAAG)* to understand precisely what the testing covers. You will find that you will be tested on questions concerning Literal Comprehension and Critical and Inferential Comprehension.

You will, upon further investigation, find that questions in this section seek to elicit, in 100- to 200-word readings, reading comprehension, identification of details in the reading, organizational issues, and identification of main ideas within the passage.

Further, you may be asked to identify premise, inference, fact, opinion and assumptions within the passage. To study for this section, I encourage you once again to:

- Seek out *LearningPlus*.

- Locate a college freshman English 101 or 102 textbook and use the Reading Comprehension section of the text to refresh, review and practice critical reading skills.

10

- Locate a tenth grade grammar book. They can be found at local high schools, libraries and school boards. Again, seek out the Reading Comprehension sections to review and restudy the critical reading skills identified in the *TAAG* on Praxis I.

Writing Skills

In the Writing section of the Praxis I you will, in sixty minutes, be asked to answer forty-five multiple choice questions and one essay. You will be asked to:

- Identify usage errors in multiple choice questions.

- Make sentence corrections in multiple choice format.

- Write an essay.

Concerning essay writing, we again need to review the basics. Essentially, the writing test pushes you towards generating an essay that follows the technical rules of writing. You may be asked to write about a number of question topics such as education, sports or hobbies.

When you approach the essay section, you must remember organization, organization and organization is the key to success. I use a method of organization called the tripartite hypothesis with the five body paragraphs. This method generates a response that, while a little clichéd, is very organized and structured.

For example, if you are asked the question, "What do you think your education has done for your life?", your response might be, "I think my education has prepared me for living in today's modern world, exposed me to critical thinking skills and taught me to enjoy learning." Now, structure a brief outline of your response.

I.   Statement of your hypothesis.

II.   Discussion of how your education has taught
       you to live in today's modern world.
       a. Examples

III.   Discussion of critical thinking skills.

IV.   Discussion of how you enjoy learning.
       a. Examples

V.   Conclusion: Restatement of hypothesis
       through evidence presented.

Other tips include:

- **Write neatly.** Make the reader happy to pick up your work.

- **Generate a brief outline.** While not graded, it will have an impact on the reader. Follow your outline.

- **Be brief.** Don't generate pages of response. I maintain the three-page rule with my students. If you can't say it in three pages, restate it.

- **Be positive.** Do not take the negative tone or side of an argument.

- **Make use of compound sentence structure** at least fifty percent of the time. A compound sentence is a sentence put together with a coordinating conjunction like *and*, *but*, *or* and *also*. For instance: "I needed to be with my friends in school *and* in my classes."

- **Make use of simple sentence structure** thirty percent of the time. Simple sentences are simply subject, noun and verb. For instance: "I enjoyed school very much."

- **Make use of compound complex sentence structure** at least twenty percent of the time. A compound complex sentence has subordinating conjunctions and independent clauses combined with coordinating conjunctions. For instance: "However, as I approach college I find that my high school education prepared me for college and trained me for life."

- **Do not make grammatical errors.**

I also recommend the following study materials for this section of the Praxis I:

- *LearningPlus.*

- *Praxis I TAAG.* This particular *TAAG* covers many topics included in the writing portion of the Praxis I.

- Practice, practice and practice some more.

Chapter 3

Praxis II

Praxis II Overview

Praxis II is the test required for certification in many states throughout the country. It is specific to either your grade level of certification or your content area. For some the Praxis II will be a test of both pedagogy and content. For others it is just a test of content for your certification area. Praxis II will be discussed in greater detail further in this text.

The Praxis II is usually taken prior to and after completion of a teacher certification program. However, some schools in some states require passing the Praxis II exam prior to gaining entry into senior block classes or teacher education in general.

What You Need to Know About the Tests

Praxis II is a criterion referenced test of your training as an educator for your particular state. All tests were developed by Educational Testing Services (ETS). Numerous educators in your state participated in the review and validation of the content categories and test questions for your state. The tests were designed to assess the minimal content knowledge needed for a beginning teacher in each field.

The tests are criterion referenced, which means scores do not reflect your performance as compared to the performance of other students who took the tests. Rather, your scores reflect your performance with respect to a standard established by educators from your state's Professional Standards Board.

The number of questions varies for each test and the number of items in each content category varies as well. The number of questions, along with each content category, is listed in the Praxis *Tests at a Glance (TAAG)* booklet for each field. For each test taken, you will receive a total test score based on a scaled score for your test field. The passing score for each field differs. Passing scores are listed in the Praxis booklet called *Understanding Your Praxis Scores.*

The content categories or subareas are weighted differently as indicated in your Praxis *Tests at a Glance (TAAG)* booklet. Therefore, different categories may be represented by a different number of test questions.

Testing Requirements

In order to meet the testing requirement for a particular certification area, you are required to pass only the test(s) in that area. For example, in Georgia the tests required of an elementary teacher are test codes 20012 and 10016. Once you have passed a test, you are not required to take that test again. If two tests are required for your field, you must pass both tests. However, if you pass one test and fail the other, you are only required to retake the test that you did not pass.

Each state requires different scores for passing as well as different test codes for each certification area. You may be asked to take one, two, three or even five tests depending on your state's requirements and your specific certification area. Refer to either your local board of education or the ETS Registration Bulletin to determine what will apply to you in your state.

Also note that the tests are divided into sessions that also indicate start times. The three sessions are coded 10, 20 and 30. For example, test 10016 begins with 10, so that session starts at

7:30 a.m. Test 20012 begins with 20, so that session starts at 10:15 a.m., 10:30 a.m. or 10:45 a.m. Test 30523 begins with 30, so that session starts at 2:15 p.m., 2:30 p.m. or 2:45 p.m. You'll find out what your start times are when your seating ticket comes in the mail. At any rate, arrive at least thirty minutes prior to your testing start time.

Passing the Praxis II

You can pass this test in one of two ways. The first way is to meet the officially published test minimum scores for your state. The second way is to meet a composite test score. A composite score is the sum of your scores if you take multiple tests. Not all states allow the composite method of passing the test. Just like the Praxis I composite method, if your state requires multiple tests for Praxis II, you can fail one of the tests and pass the second. If you live in a composite score state, you can add the two scores for a passing composite test score.

Chapter 4

Preparing for the Praxis II

The remainder of this book deals exclusively with the Praxis II exam and strategies to help you be successful when taking this test.

Praxis II asks questions about teaching or about the content areas in your field. It requires you to think about the content of the test from a process point of view.

How Do You Prepare?

The Praxis II is a very different form of testing that requires a different form of preparation. You may be tempted to memorize everything in your textbooks, or every educational theory you have studied—don't do this! These methods are just not productive or useful to your study. Remember, your test's format is specific to your content area or pedagogy required by your certification area.

Instead think about a framework as you approach this test. This framework couches your study methods, test-taking strategies and the way you think about each of the questions on the test. The framework looks like this:

- **Remember holistic.** This is a test of the sum total of your training as a teacher. All of the questions are tied to each other. Nothing stands alone.

- **Remember that each question asks about the process of teaching.** Every question will come from one of the following areas:

  - Planning—How you plan the lesson.

  - Execution—How you teach the lesson.

  - Assessment—How you assess the success of your lesson.

  - Modifications—How you change your lesson after you analyze your assessment.

Now, while thinking within this framework, examine the question, "How would you teach *Where The Wild Things Are?*" This question implies that you must show how you plan such a lesson. However, a complete response works through each component of the teaching process. Another example is the question, "Why did Mr. Tyler's lesson plan fail?" This question asks you to look specifically at how the execution of the lesson failed. To answer this question completely and correctly we have to know what happened in his planning and how he assessed what the students learned after the lesson. The processes of what came before and after execution of his lesson make your response the most complete reflection of the Praxis goal of assessing your teaching ability.

Test Question Formats

The Praxis II exam employs multiple choice, constructed response or reading comprehension questions in varying amounts.

18

Multiple Choice

In the multiple choice format, you can expect the following:

- **Vignette style.** The vignette test questions ask you to look at scenarios in education ranging from brief paragraphs to longer case studies that require your analysis and evaluation. This form of question is found on testing for the P-12 certification areas, elementary or early childhood certification areas, and the Principles of Learning and Teaching certification areas. For instance: "Mr. Tyler used a standardized test to assess his reading comprehension lesson for his seventh grade multilevel classroom. In this form of assessment he had several students who, while hard workers, still performed poorly. How might Mr. Tyler improve his assessment to better accommodate those students who might struggle with reading comprehension?"

- **Direct response style.** The direct response question primarily focuses on your content knowledge. Questions in this format ask, for instance, "What doctrine did the United States follow that excluded the Europeans from becoming entangled in Western hemispheric treaties?" or, "Who is buried in Grant's tomb?" Of course, there is only one answer for this single strand question. This form of question is found primarily in testing for the secondary certification areas and somewhat in testing for the P-12 certification areas.

- **Null value style.** The null value question asks you to look at the opposite way of answering a question. Questions may be phrased like, "When looking at this subset of disabled students, which would not be an appropriate accommodation?" This type of question is found throughout testing for all certification areas.

- **Reading comprehension style.** This style will ask you to look at a passage and answer questions concerning it. Again, this type of question is found throughout testing for all certification areas. The reading comprehension style question can be in a vignette form or be concerned with content manipulation. Reading comprehension style questions can be found in testing for the P-12 certification areas, secondary certification areas and Principles of Learning and Teaching certification areas.

Constructed Response

Examinees who take the constructed response tests are given a specified amount of time to write a response to an assigned topic, solve a mathematics or science problem, demonstrate listening or speaking competence in a foreign language, etc.

The constructed response exercise provides examinees the opportunity to demonstrate how well they support their ideas with specific examples and relevant details where appropriate, to demonstrate understanding of all parts of the equation, and to organize ideas in a logical sequence.

This form of testing is found throughout testing for all certification areas and may or may not apply to your state or certification. Numbers of questions can vary from only one question to as many as six depending on your state's requirements.

Developing Test-Taking Strategies

For the different types of questions you may face on the Praxis II, be prepared to employ strategies specific to the question format. Here are some suggestions.

Common Sense Test Taking

There are timeless test-taking strategies that can be applied to any testing situation. These have been handed down through the years and work quite well if applied together and carefully to the testing situation. They are what I call the common sense methods towards success.

- **Read all questions very carefully.** Be looking for the questions that ask for the "converse" response. A converse response question is a question that for all purposes you will glean as you are taking the test. A question like, "Which response is not...?" and "Which is most likely to be the opposite of...?"

- **If you guess,** do not change your first guess response. It is usually correct.

- **Understand what type of test you are taking.** You may or may not need to answer all of the questions to get a good score. However, leave nothing blank on the Praxis II. You are not penalized for guesses. If you are unsure, guess rather than not respond at all.

- **If the test is organized into sections,** start with the section with which you are most comfortable. This will save time and get your cognitive net warmed up. For example, a test taker may be most comfortable with the Social Studies section of the Curriculum Instruction and Assessment test, and find that the interwoven interdisciplinary nature of the questions help in other sections of the exam.

- **For reading comprehension questions,** do not read the paragraph. Use the questions asked after the paragraph to search for the information within the paragraph. The questions tell you what to look for and what the questions want to know. Remember that this is a test of your teaching skill and knowledge of your content area, not your reading skills. Do not spend time reading and re-reading passages. This takes time and is the primary place people lose the race against the clock.

- **Narrow your choices to three selections, then guess.** If you can get your choices down to three selections, you have improved your chances of getting the question correct to a one in three chance.

- **Look for key words or specific interrogatives in your questions.** For example, specific orientation of subject, noun and verbs or specific interrogatives such as *which*, *how many* and *who* allow you to scan the questions quickly and efficiently.

Multiple Choice Tests

- **Follow directions.** It is very important to listen to any instructions from the testing proctors, and follow all directions. This includes the oral directions read by the test administrators and any written directions in the test booklet. In particular, pay attention to time suggestions and directions concerning how to progress through the exam.

- **Pace your work.** Allow one minute average per multiple choice question. The number of questions varies for each test. Each test session may be one or two hours long. Before starting a test, flip through the booklet to determine the number of questions. Then determine the pace at which you should answer each question. Sixty questions in one hour allows for one question per minute.

- **Read carefully.** Do not try to speed up by skimming directions or by reading the test questions too quickly. To avoid missing important information and instructions, read the directions, test questions, and response options thoroughly.

- **Determine the "best answer."** Since the test questions call for the "best answer," you should read and evaluate all answer choices before deciding which is best. I recommend a method I call thoughtful elimination. If you can positively eliminate at least two from the selection, and can make a selection from the remaining three, go with that selection and do not change it. Statistically you are most likely to have selected the correct response.

- **Guess wisely.** Test scores are based on the number of correct answers. There is no additional penalty for guessing. For questions about which you are unsure, use your knowledge and background in the content area to eliminate as many answer choices as possible and then guess among the remaining ones.

- **Mark your answers carefully.** Answer sheets are scored electronically; it is critical that you mark your answers clearly, carefully, and completely. You may use any available space in the test booklet for notes, but all answers must be clearly marked on the answer sheet. If you skip a test question, be sure to skip the corresponding row of answer choices on the answer sheet.

- **Have a strategy for handling reading passages.** Some test questions may be based on reading passages. Go to the questions first and understand what they are asking. Make use of the subject, noun and verb in each question to provide for better skimming of reading sections.

- **Estimate.** Many test questions ask for calculations based on numerical information. When dealing with this kind of question, it is often helpful to estimate the answer before reading the response options. It is not always necessary to perform a detailed calculation to answer the question correctly. For instance, "Five percent of 95 = x." Obviously the answer must be close to or around five.

- **Check accuracy.** Use any remaining time at the end of the test session to check the accuracy of your work. Go back to test questions with which you had difficulty and verify your answers. Again, check your answer sheet to ensure that you have marked answers accurately and completely and have erased any changed answers and stray marks.

- **Use the Page Balancing technique.** In this technique students are encouraged to put questions they are not able to immediately answer at the bottom of the test booklet as they progress through the test. This is done for two reasons, the first being an immediate map of the test as the test progresses. Students will not be hunting for unanswered questions in the booklet since the questions will be placed at the bottom of the booklet for immediate access. This saves and maximizes time.

The second reason is tied to the holistic nature of the test. Since all of the questions are intertwined, students can expect that as they progress through the test they will be queued to other answers as they are exposed to other questions. Placing the questions at the bottom of the page keeps these questions at the forefront of the test taker's mind.

Constructed Response Tests

When approaching the constructed response test question, you must first compose an outline specific to the type and purpose of the essay question asked of you.

Constructed response questions are represented in two forms of essay questions. The first is concerned with content-related material, the second with pedagogy. Understanding the difference between the two predicates will help you determine how to answer the question.

1. Content Constructed Response

A content question might be, "Why did Truman use the atomic bomb to end the Pacific theater of the war?" Note that this question does not ask how to teach, or what is wrong with this teaching model or how to improve teaching strategies for maximum absorption. Indeed, this question seeks to elicit knowledge of content. A possible response might be, "Truman's use of the atomic bomb saved American lives, scared the Russians out of China, and cut as much as a year from the island hopping campaign." Again note the manipulation of content. This is called a tripartite hypothesis. The brief outline that follows shows how to organize the information into an effective response.

25

I.   Statement of your hypothesis.

II.   Discussion of how the atomic bomb saved
        American lives.
        a. Examples or information.

III.   Discussion of how the atomic bomb scared the
        Russians out of China.
        a. Examples or information.

IV.   Discussion of how the atomic bomb cut the island
        hopping campaign by one year.
        a. Examples or information.

V.   Conclusion: Restatement of hypothesis through
        evidence presented.

2. Pedagogic Constructed Response

Now let's look at a pedagogic essay question. A pedagogic essay question looks at the teaching process. An example of a pedagogic question is, "How would you teach *Where the Wild Things Are* to a fifth grade multilevel classroom?"

This question asks you to address the reflective process of teaching. In order to respond you must address the teaching framework in its entirety. A possible response hypothesis might look like this: "I would teach *Where the Wild Things Are* using TGT teaching strategies and heterogeneous grouping."

The response would be organized around the teaching framework discussed in the How Do You Prepare section in Chapter 4. See the outline on the following page.

I.   Hypothesis

II.   Planning issues—How I would plan such a lesson.

III. Execution issues—How I would teach such a lesson.

IV.   Assessment issues—How I would test students.

V.   Modification issues—What I would do differently next time.

Now if you add a separate section called Materials to this outline, you have the skeleton of a basic lesson plan. Look at the question again and think about it. It should begin to make some sense to you now.

3. General Tips for Passing Constructed Response Questions

- **Write neatly.** Make the reader happy to pick up your work.

- **Generate a brief outline.** While not graded, it will have an impact on the reader. Follow your outline when generating your written response.

- **Be brief.** Don't generate pages of response. I maintain the three-page rule with my students. If you can't say it in three pages, restate it.

- **Be positive.** Do not take the negative tone or side of an argument.

- **If you are working on an essay test**, practice making outlines and writing from outlines prior to taking the exams.

- **Make use of compound sentence structure** at least fifty percent of the time. A compound sentence is a sentence put together with a coordinating conjunction like *and, but, or* and *also*. For instance: "I needed to be with my friends in school and in my classes."

- **Make use of simple sentence structure** thirty percent of the time. Simple sentences are simply subject, noun, and verb. For instance: "I enjoyed school very much."

- **Make use of compound complex sentence structure** at least twenty percent of the time. A compound complex sentence has subordinating conjunctions and independent clauses combined with coordinating conjunctions. For instance: "However, as I approach college I find that my high school education prepared me for college and trained me for life."

- **Do not make grammatical errors.**

- **Read directions carefully.** Understand the requirements of the test instructions. If there is a choice of questions, choose the topic you can answer most knowledgeably. If there are two or more questions in a series, decide the best order in which to answer the questions.

- **Pace your activities.** Know the total amount of time allowed for the questions, and determine the number and types of questions on the test. Allow time to read each question and to plan, write, and review your answers.

- **Write your response.** In responding to a constructed response question, be clear, concise, and accurate. A longer response or an essay should answer the question completely, include appropriate concepts and terminology, provide evidence to support and amplify general statements and have a cohesive structure.

- **Use a blue or black ink pen to write your responses.**

- **Review your response.** Go back and evaluate your responses for content, clarity, and accuracy.

General Tips for Test Day

- Try to find a list of testing objectives in your *Tests at a Glance* from the ETS. The objectives tell you exactly what the test will target and thus tells you what to study. I have even seen testing objectives that tell the percentage each objective is weighted in the exam.

- Study the test by sections and not as a whole and always ask yourself, "What is this material linked to... and how is it connected?" By creating these links in your cognitive net you expand your ability to access the net at different points and with greater accuracy.

- Look at the content you are being tested on as a body of knowledge, not as individual, separate details. In your mind, be able to identify what a word, subject or event has to do with an era, larger subject or overall event. A timeline, pneumonic device or other aids will serve this function well.

- Remember to watch the clock. Most of the Praxis exams have 120 questions to be answered in 120 minutes. That works out to one minute per question. The number one complaint about the Praxis II is "I ran out of time." Do not let this happen to you. Watch the clock and look at the suggestions below.

Time Management Strategies

Remember that time management is the single biggest obstacle and arguably the most important element you can control during the test. Time management can make the difference between passing and failing this exam.

I call this first strategy the quarter hour method. First find out how many questions are on your test. Most multiple choice tests in the Praxis series have 120 questions with a time limit of two hours. Given that formula, you will need to answer one question per minute to stay on track. You can't keep this pace throughout the test; however, as you move through the test, you will find that some questions are answered more easily than others. Now, using the quarter hour method you divide the number of questions by eight, since there are eight quarter-hour segments in two hours. (120 minutes divided by fifteen minutes equals eight quarter-hour segments.) Given this figure and the number of questions (120), you determine that in every quarter hour you must answer a minimum of fifteen questions.

This method gives you a pace and a means of knowing where you should be at what time on the clock. At the very least, at every quarter hour you should be at question 15, question 30, question 45 and question 60 and so on. If you are on question 15 you should be on minute 15 on the clock. If you are on question 23 you should be at minute 23. Now, using this method, if you are on minute 22 and working on question 12 you are behind and need to pick up the pace. If you are on minute 23 and working on question 25 you are ahead and can ease up and spend that extra time on those harder questions.

The second strategy is really simple. As you are taking the test, take off your watch. It's that simple. Test takers become so absorbed in what the test is doing to them that they ignore the most important aspect of this test—time. Now, think about it. You put on a watch this morning. When was the last time you looked at your watch today? Now imagine yourself during the test, completely absorbed, stressed and worried about passing this test. The last thing you are going to think about is checking your watch. Take off your watch and put it on your desk. Now it has become an entity you have to deal with. Indeed, if you use this method, your watch is in your way, in your line of vision and in your thoughts as you move through the test. This will keep you watching the most important element of this test—time.

Chapter 5

How to Study for the Praxis II

The question of how to study is inevitably tied to what to study. First and foremost, you should not collect every textbook or scour the web for study guides. This is a fruitless process since first you must discover what to target in those materials. Approach your study materials logically and with the testing objectives in mind. Consider the following tips while gathering and studying materials.

ETS Study Materials

Collect study materials that are published by the ETS. They publish many study guides, including *TAAGs (Tests at a Glance);* make it a point to find them. Any question you can get or sample questions you can find published by ETS will be superior to other study guides and closely related to questions you may see on the test.

You can find ETS study guides and *TAAGs* online at www.teachingandlearning.org. You can also pick up *TAAGs* typically at universities or colleges with teacher education programs. To find out if a study guide has been published by the ETS for your certification area, check the back cover of the ETS registration bulletin for specifics on availability and prices. The ETS publishes new study guides all the time, so check frequently. Prices for these study guides can range from $15 to $50.

Now, when selecting *TAAGs* for study, you want to look specifically for your testing areas and content. There is a separate *TAAG* for each test code. Therefore, in order to select the relevant *TAAGs* you must first determine which test code your state requires for your area of certification. Because there are such great differences between each state's certification requirements, you will find that, for instance, test code 0011 and 0012 will be very different for each state. However, both test elementary or early childhood education. The questions in each overlap and are specifically relevant to your test taking. You will find overlap in the secondary certification areas, professional certification areas and P-12 certification areas.

Look carefully at multiple *TAAGs*. Instead of just 10 to 12 questions, you may find 50 to 100 questions—all from ETS and all directly relevant to your study. Only some of the questions in *TAAGs* outside of your testing area are relevant to you, so pick them with your specific content and grade levels in mind.

After you have found the *TAAG* for your particular test, you will need to immediately look for a page in the *TAAG* called the "Substantive Test Summary." This section of the *TAAG* will provide you with percentage information about the test if you look carefully and critically at the information. This page includes some summary information about the test, such as the number of questions and the minutes allowed for your test. More importantly, there is a breakdown of the test with approximate weightings of the test. For instance, the *TAAG* summary page for the test coded 0016 has a pie chart that is broken into the six components of the test.

Area one is worth 35%, two 20%, three 10%, four 10%, five 10% and six 15%. This not only tells you the weighting of the test, but also precisely what you need to study. The areas that compose the majority of the test, in this instance, are areas one, two and six. Now you can look further into the *TAAG* and see the testing objectives. Area one deals with reading instruction, two deals with math instruction and six deals with professional issues in elementary education. You now know what topics you need to review.

Testing Objectives: Creating a Testing Grid Map

Within the *TAAG* are some testing objectives, and, combined with the major objectives I have already described, you have enough material to build a testing grid map. This tool helps narrow down what to study and what to eliminate. An example of such a grid follows. The left hand column represents the basis of the Praxis II assessment of your teacher training and stated Praxis II testing objectives. In the right hand columns, you will write down everything in your training that satisfies the listed objectives in your program of study. These spaces may be filled with textbook titles, teaching experiences, field experiences, college courses, etc. As you move through objectives in this fashion, you may find one or two areas in your program of study or college experience that you definitely want to study and review. This process helps you select and use those materials that are specific to your studies and your test.

The following is an example of this grid building process. The major objectives are found on the left side of the grid and the spaces you fill in are immediately next to the objectives. For this example, Home Economics, the major objectives are supported by the minor objectives below.

KNOWLEDGE & SKILLS TESTED				
I. The Family				
Family structures: single parent, nuclear, extended, and blended families, as well as the single individual				

Family stages: the beginning and expanding family and retirement				
Family functions: the education and development of family members, including transmission of heritage, behavior modeling, and consumer education; and the physical and psychological support of family members, including parenting, supplying basic needs, fostering self-worth, maintaining stable relations, and providing recreation				
Factors affecting family relationships: multiple roles; communication patterns, including conflict prevention and resolution; and interactions with society, including changing roles and lifestyles				

II. Human Development				
Theories of development: Gesell and Ilg, Havinghurst, Erikson, and Piaget				
Development tasks and processes: social, physical, psychological/emotional, and intellectual				
Variations in development requiring special resources and responses: handicapped and gifted conditions, drug and alcohol abuse, teenage pregnancies, and teen suicide				
III. Management				
Management theory: work simplification, time management, and organization of activities				

Management processes and techniques: goal-setting; decision-making strategies; assessing and using resources; strategies for changes; and the identification and clarification of family values, goals, and standards in management decisions				
IV. Consumer Economics				
Consumer rights and responsibilities: legal and ethical considerations				
Societal influences on consumer decisions: impact of marketing, identification of wants versus needs, effect of the economy, conservation and environmental concerns				

Consumer resources for decision-making: private and government agencies providing assistance and information, published materials				
Selection of services and products: health-care services, child-care services, and repair services; household materials and equipment, automobiles, toys				
Financial planning and management: family budgets, credit, investments, insurance, retirement planning, savings and checking accounts				
Consumer protection: labels, warranties, guarantees, government agencies, and consumer advocate groups				

V. Nutrition and Food				
Factors influencing nutritional needs: gender, age, activity				
Functions and sources of nutrients: calcium for bone-building, iron for blood cells, and vitamin A for eyes and skin				
Nutritional guidelines: RDA, USRDA, Dietary Guidelines for Americans, USDA Daily Food Guide				
Related health problems: anorexia, bulimia, obesity, and diabetes, as well as prevention and treatment strategies				
Sociocultural aspects of food: considerations related to ethics, morals, religion, and ethnicity, and the physiological and psychological satisfactions of food				

Meal/food management: order of preparation, type of meal service related to food choices and number of people to be served, preparation time, money available				
Food selection and purchase: types of food choices and number of people to be served, preparation time, money available				
Food preparation: food science principles involved in undercooking, over handling, additives, and proper cooking temperatures; and selection and use of equipment involving heat conductivity, energy conservation, and time/person management				
Food storage and preservation: the cleanliness of food handlers, surroundings, and utensils; and proper				

storage environment, new preservation techniques such as irradiation, and the shelf life of products				
VI. Clothing and Textiles				
Wardrobe management: planning, selection, and purchase; clothing construction; and the care of clothing				
Textiles: types and characteristics of fibers, production and properties of fabrics				
VII. Housing				
Housing: functions of housing, types of housing, factors that affect consumer housing decisions, and interior design factors				
VII. Family and Consumer Sciences Education				
Philosophical and professional concerns: improvement for the				

quality of life; elimination of sex-role stereotypes: preparation of both males and females for dual-careers as homemaker/wage earner; integration of the cognitive, affective, and psychomotor skills necessary to function effectively as an individual and as a family member; role of professional organizations in family and consumer sciences education				
Characteristics of consumer/homemaking education and occupational family and consumer sciences education				
Planning, implementation, and evaluation: use of community advisory committees in planning programs; laboratory setting and demonstration methods; role of youth organizations such as FHA/HERO; career education; impact of				

legislation; meeting the needs of special students; appropriate assessment techniques, such as use of observation and quality checklists in laboratory settings			

As you can see, this is a grid prepared for Home Economics testing. Follow the model to create a grid for your area. List the test objectives in the left hand column of the grid. Think back over your classes, textbooks, classroom assignments, and field experiences that address these objectives and list them in the spaces next to your objectives. After you have completed section 1, you will probably discover that one textbook, or several field experiences, specifically apply to your studies. Hopefully, you will have kept your college textbooks or know where to get them. You now know what textbooks to look for and what materials to review in those textbooks. You now have a road map to follow when looking at the vast amount of material you could study. This material can include other study guides on the market, from a variety of publishing companies such as Arco, Baron's, Princeton Review, Arrow, and of course, ETS. It is usually easy to find these types of study guides on the web at www.amazon.com and www.barnesandnoble.com.

Formulating a Study Plan

- **Review the test content categories and content descriptions.** They are the core of the testing program and are the most helpful study tools available to determine the strengths and weaknesses in your content knowledge.

- **Use the content description information** on your score report (if you are retaking the test). This information will further help you determine the areas in which you should focus most of your studies.

- **Review class notes and textbooks.** The Praxis subject tests are designed to cover a broad range of knowledge, usually acquired throughout a teacher preparation program. Review the appropriate *Tests at a Glance* booklet and find corresponding relevant material in your class notes and textbooks for review.

- **Take additional courses.** Consult with your advisor and, on his or her recommendation, take courses that will help you strengthen those areas where your content knowledge is weak.

- **Form or join a study group.** Study groups are most effective once you have identified the test content categories with which you are less familiar. If you have a very specific need or area of weakness, a study group with a narrower focus or a tutor may be more appropriate.

- **Avoid "cramming" in the final days before the test.** Plan to spend at least six weeks studying for this exam. Praxis II tests cover a broad range of content. They are not the type of tests for which last minute "cramming" is effective. A review of all your appropriate subject matter and education coursework is necessary. Allow plenty of time for your preparation; with the broad range of knowledge tested, this is not the type of test for which "cramming" the week or night before the test is effective.

Ancillary Resources

State standards and measures for meeting curriculum are excellent resources for Praxis II preparation. Each state has adopted guidelines for each grade level and content category. The standards will show you how to teach a topic, how to assess a topic, how to plan a topic and when to teach a topic. This provides the Praxis II test taker with invaluable information for study since, remember, you are taking a test about teaching. And the standards and measures of each state are about... teaching!

Yet another interesting alternative study source, especially if you are testing in a content area, are the actual textbooks of those grade levels you will be teaching. Take for instance the secondary English test of literature. What better source to review than the actual anthologies of the tenth, eleventh and twelfth grades to see precisely what material to cover, review and study.

Physiological Preparation

I am constantly amazed at the lack of attention paid to physiological preparation for test taking. Students often ignore advice given by the most respected athletes in the world, that advice being, "the body is a machine and must be prepared for the activity you demand from it." What is true for the sports world is true for academics; students must pay attention to the demands of the body in preparing for an exam.

Often we rely upon the clichéd portrayal of studying: students burning the midnight oil, consuming huge quantities of caffeine, eating inappropriate meals, if at all, getting no exercise and ignoring the body's demands for sleep. The body, especially the brain, needs three things to run at peak performance: oxygen, energy and rest. What we can do to improve the body's reception of these critical components will have an impact on how the body performs in the academic arena. Some widely accepted basic tips follow.

- **No red meat or heavy meals** with complex fibers, fats or oils the night before or the day of the exam.

- **No smoking the day of the exam.** Smoking puts carbon dioxide and carbon monoxide into the bloodstream. Both of these gases more readily bond with blood hemoglobin, depriving the body of this important gas and, thus, decreasing the amount of oxygen that goes into the brain and body. Also, no smoking the night before, if it can be avoided.

- **No alcohol the night before or the day of the exam.**

- **Try to aerobically exercise,** at least 30 minutes daily, for the week prior to the exam, and on the day of the exam. This increases the body's ability to take and use oxygen as well as improves metabolism.

- **No caffeine the day of or before the exam.** No coffee, diet cola or tea. This is false energy that will not help your body and will quickly dissipate.

- **Try to eat heavy natural carbohydrate meals** (not candy bars) the night before and the day of the exam. Foods heavy with natural fibers, oils and simple fats are examples of "good" foods to eat (for example, raw vegetables, brown rice, pasta with light, simple sauces, whole grain breads, fish, skinned and broiled chicken, etc.).

- **Try to get up at least two hours before the test** and get at least eight hours of sleep before the exam. Do not stay up all night.

- **Do not "hunch" over the test.** Sit up straight, breathe deeply and give your body the oxygen needed to function well.

- **Do not panic.** The bane of all test takers, a panic attack eliminates most clear thought processes and makes the test taking experience both miserable and unsuccessful.

Intellectual Preparation

The final area that needs to be addressed is the correct method of studying. Intellectually, a test taker must finally prepare what material goes into the brain and how that material gets there. Correctly studying, not cramming, can ease the stress of studying, test preparation and test taking. Studying materials for the exam in an order that best facilitates comprehension and retention of materials is crucial to effective preparation. By using what materials exist and rendering them into an easily intellectually grasped form, a test taker can begin to get a handle on the vast amounts of material needed for an examination. By using materials from testing sources, an observant and attentive test taker can piece together a formidable plan of attack.

These tips are designed to expand the cognitive net of information and increase the mind's ability to access material in one's cognitive net more readily and with greater accuracy. The cognitive net is, psychologists have shown, the method by which the human brain stores and retrieves information as it is needed. Think literally of a large fish net. Each knot represents a parcel of information on a subject. The rope between the knots represents an intellectual link. This link represents learning beyond rote memorization.

As you increase the number of knots and links, you increase the overall size and relative success of your mind's ability to extract and use information from the cognitive net. As a test taker makes more and more connections in their cognitive net, intellectual preparedness increases for that test, and any other test.

As we look back over the testing experience there is a common thread that should be apparent. That thread is the assumption that you are at the testing site at an appropriate point and time in your academic experience. There are no tips, no magic formulas or universal rules to follow when taking a test. Test preparation is left up to the test taker and that person's ability to adequately prepare and be prepared. Suggestions can be made to help prepare a test taker for a test; however, it is up to the test taker to adequately prepare throughout the classes that make up a program of study. It is ultimately up to the student to develop the framework necessary for a cognitive net to be formed.

I encourage you to review the suggestions offered here, discuss them with your advisor, and employ those that are best suited to your needs.

Chapter 6

Examples of Praxis II Questions

Multiple Choice

The questions below represent the styles you may expect to see on the Praxis II. Where various forms arise I have identified them to direct your attention to the change of style and direction of the questions. Do not let the content of the questions concern you. Just review the format and the way in which the interrogative is directed at you.

Direct Response Formats

1. What problems does a person with a disability encounter when interacting with the environment?
    a. impairment
    b. at-risk
    c. handicap
    d. learning disability

2. The term at-risk is most often applied to:
    a. children with a history of school failure
    b. secondary students
    c. infants and preschoolers
    d. middle school students

3. Since 1975, the number of children and youth who receive special education has:
    a. increased
    b. decreased
    c. remained stable
    d. not been counted

4. Approximately what percentage of the school-age population do children with handicaps represent?
   a. 3
   b. 6
   c. 9
   d. 12

5. Most children who receive special education services are:
   a. infants and toddlers
   b. between the ages of 3 and 9
   c. between the ages of 10 and 17
   d. over age 15

6. According to the *12th Annual Report to Congress*, the largest category of children receiving special education is children with:
   a. learning disabilities
   b. mental retardation
   c. physical and other health impairments
   d. speech and language impairment

7. The "typical" child who receives special education in the U.S. is a:
   a. 7-year-old female with mild mental retardation who spends the entire day in a special class
   b. 9-year-old male with speech and language impairment who spends part of the school day in the regular classroom and part in a resource room
   c. 9-year-old male with learning disabilities who spends part of the school day in the regular classroom and part in a resource room
   d. 10-year-old female with emotional disturbance who spends most of the school day in a special class

8. Research on labeling indicates that the effects of labeling are:
   a. usually negative
   b. usually positive
   c. inconclusive and contradictory
   d. educationally helpful

9. A possible benefit of labeling is that it:
   a. helps make the special needs of exceptional children more visible
   b. protects children with handicaps from situations in which they are not able to compete
   c. focuses attention on the negative aspects of the child
   d. tells teachers exactly what level of performance should be expected from the child

Vignette Style

10. Mr. Malloy, a regular class math teacher, is concerned about teaching Jessica, a special education student, because he does not know her classification. How would it help Mr. Malloy to know Jessica's classification?
    a. It would not help Mr. Malloy know how to teach Jessica.
    b. It would help Mr. Malloy select reinforcers for Jessica.
    c. It would help Mr. Malloy design a behavior management system for Jessica.
    d. It would help Mr. Malloy choose a peer tutor for Jessica.

11. The 14th Amendment to the U.S. Constitution guarantees:
    a. employment opportunities for all handicapped adults
    b. freedom of speech
    c. equal protection under the law
    d. freedom of the press

12. The Education for Handicapped Children Act is referred to as P.L.
    a. 93-380
    b. 94-142
    c. 87-276
    d. 89-10

Null Value Style

13. Which is NOT guaranteed by the Education for All Handicapped Children Act?
    a. an appropriate education for gifted children
    b. an individualized education plan
    c. safeguards to protect the rights of students with handicaps
    d. a free appropriate public education

14. In regular education the school system is dictated by the curriculum, but in special education the curriculum is dictated by the:
    a. child's parents
    b. school psychologist
    c. special education teacher
    d. child's needs

15. What portion of children with handicaps receive education in the regular classroom?
    a. one-fourth
    b. one-half
    c. two-thirds
    d. three-fourths

16. The overall goal of intervention is to:
   a. cure the individual of the handicapping condition
   b. assist the individual to accept his/her limitations
   c. eliminate or reduce obstacles that impede the individual's full participation in society
   d. enable the individual to achieve minimum levels of reading and math skills

Answer Key

1. d.
2. c.
3. c.
4. a.
5. b.
6. a.
7. c.
8. c.
9. a.
10. a.
11. c.
12. b.
13. a.
14. d.
15. c.
16. c.

Reading Comprehension

Notice that this form of question seeks to elicit literal comprehension of the reading, as well as inferential issues such as opinion and overall reading comprehension. Again, remember to look at the question first and determine what the question seeks from you. Some tests will ask you to provide the type of information presented on the following pages, while other tests will ask you to evaluate large portions of an IEP or a teacher's actions during a lesson.

The psychological mechanisms that permit technology to take a dominant role in adult education are much more difficult to grasp for the casual reader. This part of the question drives me to look at adult learners in a different light than that to which I am accustomed. The adult learners, in many circumstances, are learning willingly and usually learning what they feel is important to them and their future. If the above sociological causes drive learning, then it becomes important to look at what people see as worthy of learning and what knowledge should be. If people are driven by this epistemological evaluation of knowledge, then technology is seen as a requirement for modern existence and continued success. Thus, the psychological mechanisms that drive technology in adult education settings can be tied to a fear of being left behind the rest of society (Postman, 1993). This again displays the power technology can and does wield and indicates its importance at the program planning table. Further, as technology and especially computer technology has become "institutionalized into religion, government, education and recreation," our ability as humans to be participative is tied to a "faith" in technology that diminishes our ability to question and function without it (Postman, 1993). Negative psychological consequences develop among non-technical adult learners. Such issues include computer anxiety, self-esteem issues and communication issues that stem from the inability to participate in the technology surrounding their lives (Hacker, 2000).

The key aspects of selecting educational technologies to support adult learning should accordingly and correctly be tied to understanding what kind of students the technology will impact. As I researched this part I realized there are two distinctive components to address. First is the nature of adult learners, adult learning theory and adult curriculum. Second are the practical "nuts and bolts" decisions to be made about the various elements ranging from selection of technology to the superstructure surrounding adult education settings. These questions are all part of the program planning process, yet draw responses from various locations in the literature.

The "nuts and bolts" issues surrounding selecting technology for adult education settings are tied to prioritizing and establishing agreed upon criteria (Smith & Ragan, 1993, Cashman and Rosenblatt, 1996; Jordan and Machesky, 1990). These criteria is made up of the following components:

1. How are current technologies being used?
2. What are the attitudes of the faculty, staff and administration toward the use of available technologies?
3. Do existing technologies within the institution aid the teaching and learning process?
4. Which individuals within the institution make decisions regarding information and technology?
5. If new technologies were implemented, how would the faculty, staff and administration prefer to interact with the new technologies?

6. How would these individuals choose to utilize new, emerging technologies to enhance the learning experience?
7. How should the classroom environments be configured for optimal effectiveness and creativity?
8. What individuals should be involved in this change process?

(Hamza & Alhalabi, 1999)

In addition, we must consider basic logistical elements at the various sites where technologically based learning will take place. For instance, presence of adequate electrical and electrical system needs, remote site facilitators, and adequate knowledge by the end-user of hardware and software requirements are all important. In addition, remote sites must be able to support hardware and software requirements in terms of RAM, hard drive space, printing capabilities, and chip speed.

Once the basic hardware, software, and other practical requirements are met, the other key aspects of adult learners, theory, and curriculum can be addressed. As with all adult learning, if we apply basic adult learning theory to technological implementation of instruction we come up with a checklist to follow as we progress with our program planning. If we accept that the basic tenets of adult education are based on the ideas of self-directed learning (Grow, 1991), transformative learning (Clark, 1993), and general andragogic philosophies (Knowles,

56

1984), we can see that by understanding the nature of adult learning we can better facilitate what goes into technologically based curricula. When working with adult learners, the nature of computer or Internet based learning naturally lends itself to adult learning styles and beliefs. The inherent, self-paced, self-driven format of many of the theories surrounding adult learning allow self-directed learning to flourish and provide an autonomy to the learner not present in face to face didactic situations.

1. What is the opinion of the author?
   a. Supportive of technology in education settings
   b. Negative towards technology in education settings
   c. Advocating greater use of technology
   d. Advocating greater integration of technology in adult education settings

2. Who does the author cite as a leading antagonist to technology in education?
   a. Postman
   b. Mezirow
   c. Riel
   d. Knowles

3. What are the apparent weaknesses in using technology for instruction?
   a. Lack of face to face instruction
   b. Didactic nature
   c. No thoughtful planning
   d. Lack of critical thinking skills

Essay or Critical Response

Now when looking at the essay or critical response questions, remember to determine what they are asking of you. Below are a couple of examples of what you may be asked in either of the essay formats. The pedagogy format will elicit knowledge of the process, and the content format will elicit knowledge of the subject.

Pedagogy Essay Topics

1. How would you teach *Where the Wild Things Are* to a fifth grade multilevel reading classroom, maximizing coding for reading, word recognition strategies, flexible assessment and maximizing various reading accommodations for low level readers?

2. How would you structure a math manipulative lesson for fourth graders learning how to add fractions?

Content Essay Topics

1. Why did Truman use the atomic bomb to end the Pacific theater of the war?

2. Compare and contrast the ideas of good and evil in Shakespeare's characters of Lady Macbeth and Lord Caliban.

3. Why did humans settle along the cradles of civilization?

Appendix

Self-Evaluation for Education Professionals and Students

Step 1: Interview the student and discuss the testing program and the scoring process.

Step 2: Review the test content categories.

Step 3: Determine the student's content category mastery.

Step 4: Develop a study plan.

Step 5: Help the student improve test-taking skills.

Student Profile

Your goal in completing this profile is to provide faculty at your teacher education institution with information that will be useful to them in helping you prepare to take the appropriate Praxis II exams.

General Information

Student's name:_____

Date:_____

Advisor's name:_____

Major area of study:_____

Minor area of study:_____

What is your current academic status? Circle one.

First Year   Sophomore   Junior   Senior   Graduate Student

Other_____

What type of certificate do you expect to seek?

What content area do you want to teach?

What grade do you want to teach?

Which subjects in your core curriculum did you find the most interesting?

In what state do you think you will be teaching?

Have you taken and passed all three components of the Praxis I? (State requirement will need to be confirmed.)

Is there an exemption for you on your Praxis I scores?

What is the exemption from?

Do you have a composite passing score?

Which Praxis II tests are you currently preparing to take?

Have you received the appropriate *Tests at a Glance* booklet for your test field?

Have you read the study guide and reviewed the sample question formats in the study guide?

Have you identified content categories, content components, or cover topics that are unfamiliar to you?

What course(s) are you taking or have you taken that may have included material which will be on this test? Attach additional sheets if necessary.

Course   Do you still have notes?   Old tests?   Old textbooks?

1.

2.

3.

Have you reviewed readings, notes, and books from these classes?

Have you looked at the state curriculum guides to assist you in understanding pedagogic components?

What additional questions do you have about material you have identified and reviewed?

Have you reviewed the texts of the grade levels or content you will be teaching?

Have you contacted the state you are going to teach in to identify requirements for certification?

If you have taken the Praxis, have you reviewed the grade report to develop test-taking feedback?

Have you reviewed the *TAAGs* for your area to understand weighting of your exam objectives?

What other steps have you taken to prepare for the test?

What additional information might be useful to faculty members as they help you prepare to take the test? For example, have you taken the test before? What were your total and content category scores on any previous attempt(s)?

Faculty Recommendations to the Student

1. Form a study group
2. Library references
3. Textbook references
4. Coursework recommendations

Other recommendations

Notes

Notes

Blank Grid for Mapping Testing Objectives

Objectives	Classes	Texts	Lectures	Other